In the Grove of Olives

Matthew: *Chapter 26:36—26:75*

After the Passover Meal, Jesus along with his disciples went to an orchard of olive trees called the 'Garden of Gethsemane'. Often Jesus went to the garden to escape the busy city streets and to pray. Today too he went there to pray and Judas knew where Jesus would be.

Peter, John and James had accompanied Jesus to the garden. As Jesus knew what was to happen in a little while, his heart was filled with sorrow. 'Keep me company,' Jesus said to his disciples. 'My heart is nearly breaking with sorrow and sadness.'

Soon, leaving his companions, Jesus went a little ahead in the garden to pray. 'Please Father; if it is possible spare me the suffering that is to come. Do not let me go through it. But above all I want to do what pleases you,' prayed Jesus.

Though his disciples knew that Jesus needed them but tiredness overcame them and they fell asleep. When Jesus returned after his prayers, he found them fast asleep. Gently he woke them up and said, 'Couldn't you stay awake with me for even an hour?'

Again Jesus went off to pray and when he returned he found Peter, James and John sleeping. When he woke them up the third time, Jesus said, 'Now you must wake up for I am about to be taken as a prisoner.' Then pointing in a direction, he said, 'Look! Here comes the one who has betrayed me.'

The three disciples rubbed their eyes and looked in the direction where Jesus had pointed. There they saw lanterns dangling in the hands of men and heard the dull sound of the soldiers armour as they walked. And then their eyes widened and they were filled with horror and disbelief.

Walking among the soldiers, they saw Judas Iscariot. They understood that he was the traitor about whom Jesus had spoken of during the Passover Meal. At once Judas rushed forward and kissed Jesus. It was a signal to the soldiers that this was the man they were to arrest. Judas had previously told the soldiers, 'The one that I shall kiss is the man whom you have to take! Seize him and hold him fast.'

Then Jesus said to Judas, 'Judas, do not betray the Son of Man with a kiss.' Then turning to the soldiers, Jesus asked, 'Whom do you seek?'

'Jesus of Nazareth,' the soldiers replied.

'I am he, whom you seek,' said Jesus.

At once, the soldiers rushed forward toward Jesus brandishing their swords and spears as if they were about to catch a criminal.

Seeing the soldiers rushing towards Jesus, Peter, angry, took out his sword, swung it and cut the ear of a soldier. 'Put your sword away, Peter,' said Jesus firmly. 'If I wanted to go free, I could call the armies of angels to fight for me. But I am ready to give up my life according to God's plan.'

Then, Jesus touched the wounded ear of the soldier and made it whole. The three disciples could not understand why Jesus wanted to get himself arrested. In despair and fear, they ran away. The soldiers then took their unresisting prisoner to the house of the High Priest.

Meanwhile, Peter and John had recovered themselves and went to the High Priest's house. John, who knew some of the members of the household, went inside while Peter stayed in the courtyard. Suddenly, a woman asked Peter, 'Aren't you a follower of that man?'
'No, I am not,' said Peter angrily.

As Peter crossed the courtyard, a man said, 'You are one among his followers.' Growing afraid, again, Peter said, 'I do not even know the man.' Hastily, Peter stepped out of the courtyard when another man said, 'No matter what he says, he is certainly the prisoner's follower. Hear him speak, he is from Galilee.'

‘I do not know what you are talking about. But I tell you that I do not know the man,’ Peter said angrily. Just then, the shrill voice of a cockerel was heard. At once, Peter remembered Jesus’ words that he would deny him three times before the cock crows.

As Peter looked at the calm figure of Jesus, the Lord looked at him with understanding and love. Peter could not bear it and went away crying bitterly.

Meanwhile, all night long the High Priest along with his council found Jesus guilty under false charges and decided to sentence him to death.